American Astronomer
by Mary Virginia Fox

A Book Report Biography
FRANKLIN WATTS
A Division of Grolier Publishing
New York / London / Hong Kong / Sydney
Danbury, Connecticut

Cover illustration by Marco Ventura

Photographs ©: California Institute of Technology: 27, 33, 83, 93;
Carnegie Institution of Washington: 67, 78; Corbis-Bettmann: 39, 70, 91;
Huntington Library: 2, 16, 23, 44, 46, 52, 57, 60, 74, 76, 81, 86, 87, 98, 101;
NASA: 8, 13; Yerkes Observatory: 29.

Library of Congress
Cataloging-in-Publication Data

Fox, Mary Virginia.
　　Edwin Hubble : American astronomer / by Mary Virginia Fox.
　　　　p. cm.—(A Book report biography)
　　Includes bibliographical references and index.
　　Summary: Traces the life and work of the man whose study of galax-
ies led to a new understanding of the universe.
　　ISBN 0-531-11371-X
　　1. Hubble, Edwin Powell, 1889–1953—Biography—Juvenile litera-
ture. 2. Astronomy—History—United States—Juvenile literature. 3.
Astronomers—United States—Biography—Juvenile literature. [1. Hub-
ble, Edwin Powell, 1889–1953. 2. Astronomers.] I. Title. II. Series.
QB36.H83F69 1997
520'.92—dc21
[B]　　　　　　　　　　　　　　　　　　　　　　　　　97-12098
　　　　　　　　　　　　　　　　　　　　　　　　　　　CIP
　　　　　　　　　　　　　　　　　　　　　　　　　　　AC

EDWIN HUBBLE

CONTENTS

CHAPTER ONE

THE TELESCOPE IS NAMED

On April 14, 1990, the 25,000-pound (11,340-kg) Hubble Space Telescope blasted into orbit aboard the space shuttle *Discovery* amid dazzling hopes. In spite of a faulty mirror, a mistake measured in fractions of a millimeter, the Hubble Space Telescope was seeing billions of miles farther than had ever been seen before, stretching the boundaries of our known map of space.

Because light takes so long to reach us from the outposts of space, we see distant objects not as they are but as they were millions or billions of years ago, the moment their light left on its long journey to Earth. The light from the most distant detectable objects left its source long before dinosaurs were roaming Earth.

The Hubble Space Telescope is like a time machine, showing us the early stages of the universe, when galaxies were just starting to form.

Scientists at the Kennedy Space Center continue work on the Hubble Space Telescope six months before its launch aboard the space shuttle Discovery.

We are seeing into the past of these mysterious clusters of stars and unknown space material. Astronomers are hoping to determine the age of the universe and speculate what the future has in store. They need to study the nature of deep-space phenomena such as quasars and supermassive black holes. Scientists hope that the Hubble Space Telescope will help solve the volume of puzzles that have been around since life on Earth began looking heavenward.

WHO IS HUBBLE?

But who is this man named Hubble who lent his name to this wonderful instrument that is now helping to answer some of these questions? Who is this man whose work is considered so important that since his death in 1953 it has been carried on by other great scientists?

Dr. Daniel Seeley of Harvard University ranks the theories and discoveries of Edwin Powell Hubble as "the most significant contributions to cosmology since the time of Copernicus." Stephen Hawkins, world-famous physicist, wrote of Hubble, "He changed the concept of the universe more profoundly than anyone else."

> **"He changed the concept of the universe more profoundly than anyone else."**
> **—Stephen Hawkins**

Edwin Hubble captured public interest on November 25, 1924 when an astonishing article in the *New York Times* quoted him as having found proof that certain spiral groups of stars were so distant that they were outside the boundaries of our own Milky Way galaxy. Hubble further announced that they were galaxies in their own right, containing millions of stars similar to the ones Earthlings were able to see in their own sky.

A light-year, the distance that light travels in one year, is about 6,000,000,000,000 miles (9,656,040,000,000 km). These galaxies, spiral swirls of cosmic matter that Hubble called "island universes," were millions of light-years away. Such tremendous distances challenged even the most imaginative minds.

Furthermore, he calculated that these galaxies were traveling away from us at tremendous speeds, providing evidence for the theory that the universe must at one time have been made up of a concentrated mass of matter that exploded in a "big bang" at the very instant the universe was formed. To those first reading about Hubble's finds, the planet inhabited by the human race seemed smaller than ever compared to the massive universe expanding around it.

Not everyone agreed with Hubble's findings. Certainly there were many theologians who were unwilling to accept this new concept of creation, and there were astronomers, too, who questioned his figures. Still, Hubble felt certain that with further research his findings would be recognized as fact. But he was well aware that many new discoveries would have to wait until a telescope could be built that would somehow bypass Earth's atmosphere, which causes images observed through it to shimmer and tremble. He envisioned a telescope that could fly above the atmosphere and thus avoid its distorting effects. During Hubble's lifetime, instruments were sent up by balloons, but scientists had not found ways to direct their focus accurately. They were forced to rely on powerful telescopes on mountaintops.

A SPACE TELESCOPE

Edwin Hubble wasn't the first to propose a space telescope. In 1946, Lyman Spitzer Jr., who is now an emeritus professor at Princeton University, wrote about such a "dream machine," but it was not until rockets had put the first satellites in space that anyone seriously began planning such an instrument. By the 1990s, space technology had advanced to the point where the construction and launch of such an instrument was possible, and in April 1990 the dream machine became a reality.

However, when scientists viewed the first images from the Hubble Space Telescope, they were discouraged. The images were not nearly as clear as expected. In December 1993, more than two and a half years after the launch of the Hubble Space Telescope, NASA launched the most ambitious space mission since astronauts landed on the moon. The space shuttle *Endeavor* went into orbit with a crew of seven to completely overhaul the telescope and repair the malfunctioning instruments. The mission succeeded, and the telescope now provides astronomers with exceptionally clear pictures of deep space.

The Hubble Space Telescope is actually a bus-size collection of instruments, including several kinds of telescopes and cameras. The wide-field planetary camera aboard the Hubble Space Telescope is capable of spotting a light from an ordinary two-cell flashlight at the distance of the moon. There is also a faint-object camera that is powerful enough to read a license plate from 30 miles (48 km) away. The Hubble also contains the Goddard spectroscope, the most powerful and sensitive device for analyzing ultraviolet light ever built. Because it detects only invisible ultraviolet rays, light in the visible spectrum cannot cause interference. To make these sensitive measurements possible, the Hubble's guidance system is designed to hold the focus of the telescope for up to 24 hours with a precision equal to the width of a human hair as seen from a distance of 1 mile (1.6 km).

The single most important question scientists hope the Hubble Space Telescope will answer is whether the rate of the expansion of the universe is slowing down sufficiently so that at some point

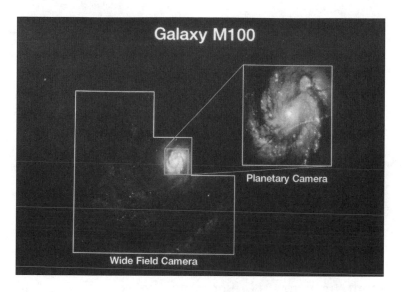

The cameras aboard the Hubble Space Telescope provide spectacular pictures of this spiral galaxy.

it will reach zero speed and collapse upon itself, or if space matter will continue to hurtle away from itself forever. This was what Hubble was trying to determine before his sudden death in 1953.

Many people lent their talents to develop the Hubble Space Telescope, but when the time came to christen the telescope, no one doubted that the honor should go to Edwin Powell Hubble. It was he who had stretched the horizons of outer space the farthest during modern times. He would have been very proud, but maybe a bit envious that he wasn't the first one to see what was out there.

CHAPTER TWO

A HOUSEFUL OF HUBBLES

Edwin Powell Hubble's ancestors immigrated to North America from England in the early seventeenth century. Galileo was the scientist of the day. With dry wit, Edwin himself explained, "Whenever there was trouble in England, one of the family left in a hurry."

Richard Hubble, the astronomer's great-grandfather, settled in raw frontier country in what is now Boone County, Missouri. He was successful as a landowner, trader, and insurance agent. At his death, he was able to leave five thousand dollars to each of his eleven children, a considerable fortune at the time.

Edwin Hubble's paternal grandfather, Martin Hubble, fought for the North during the Civil War. When the fighting was over, he advocated clemency for his former enemies, which upset his neighbors. But he had reason to sympathize;

Hubbles had fought for the Confederacy as well. There were times when they had faced each other across trenches. Honor and bravery had been displayed on both sides, facts the present generation has kept alive in collections of family letters and diaries.

THE EARLY YEARS

John Hubble, Edwin's father, married Virginia Lee James (who was known as Jennie) in the small town of Marshfield, Missouri, in 1880. Within a few years they had a son, Henry, and a daughter, Lucy. On November 20, 1889, Edwin Powell Hubble was born in Marshfield. Later, the family expanded to include six more children: Bill, Virginia, Helen, Emma, and Elizabeth, who was known as Betsy.

John Hubble, had studied law, but it was decided he could use his skills in the family insurance business to better advantage, so the family moved to the company's headquarters in Springfield, Missouri. The firm later moved John Hubble to Chicago, Illinois, where the family lived in the suburbs—first in Evanston and then Wheaton.

Such frequent moves put everyone in the family to the test of making new friends and coping with change, but as Betsy, the youngest Hubble,

Edwin (third from left) with cousins in 1900

remembers, this only helped to strengthen family ties. They spent a great deal of time together.

The family living quarters were always large and comfortable, with enough room for everyone to have his or her own bedroom. The young children were given a certain amount of freedom but were always under the watchful eyes of a stern father and a tolerant mother.

At precisely six-thirty, a half hour after John Hubble returned from his office, the dinner gong sounded, and the clan gathered for dinner. All were expected to be prompt. Two servants—a cook and a maid—helped with household chores, but each member of the family was given duties, "to give them a sense of the responsibilities of adult life," in the words of Father.

Jennie Hubble was an attractive, statuesque woman who stood almost as tall as her husband. She had light-blond hair and a ready smile that often erupted in bursts of laughter. She enjoyed entertaining, and whenever the family moved to a new location, her hospitality was soon known throughout the neighborhood.

Jennie Hubble had a special talent for settling disputes before they hit the boiling point. Only once did anyone remember Mother letting her temper fly. It was when Lucy and Henry took treats off the buffet table just before company was to be served.

Edwin was most like his mother in appearance, inheriting her elegant, almost regal manner, but lacking her sense of humor. In later life these qualities were often interpreted as aloofness.

A CHILDHOOD TRAGEDY

Even Mother's calming influence could not always maintain peace in the big, noisy family. One of Edwin's stormy encounters with his younger sister Virginia changed the character of his childhood. He and his brother Bill built an elaborate fort, complete with a plank bridge, in the backyard. Everything was painstakingly put together with bent nails and hours of patience and sweat. Virginia, who was named after her mother and considered the family favorite, had a habit of making fun of their war games. One day when she was causing more trouble than usual, Edwin shouted at her and swore that if he were a real soldier, he would shoot her through and through.

Within weeks Virginia was dead of scarlet fever. Edwin's words came back to haunt him. For a whole month he refused to come out of his room or have anything to do with the rest of the family. Meals were brought to him, and only his mother entered his room. His sisters remember that there were whispers that he was having a nervous breakdown, meaning to them that he was going crazy.

One day, without notice, he finally opened his door and joined the world around him. He seemed to have changed, growing more serious. He took on more responsibility for his brothers and sisters, especially the younger ones. He never complained about taking them to the circus and once, when he was older, to a play. His classmates teased him for being a nursemaid, but he replied that they had missed a good time.

John Hubble held strict rules on proper upbringing. Attending church was mandatory, and alcohol was never allowed in the home. When the family lived in Wheaton, Illinois, which was close to a racetrack for horses, Edwin had a hard time obeying Father's laws. No one was to attend a sporting event where betting was permitted, and no one was to have anything to do with those engaged in a sport that supported gambling.

Two of Edwin's friends, Alson and George, were hired as part-time stable boys, earning good money that they were putting aside for some mysterious trip they planned to take. They urged Edwin to join them, at least for the job. They'd let him in on their secret if he worked hard.

Edwin agreed to meet them on a Saturday morning. He managed to escape the house early enough to avoid questions, but on his return, the aroma of horse manure he had been shoveling all day told the tale. In spite of the fact that he had certainly not been gambling, a punishment was prescribed. For the next month, Edwin did his shoveling in the backyard flower garden.

Many evenings the family held their own concerts. Father played the violin. Lucy, the musical star of the family, was an accomplished pianist. Edwin and Bill played mandolins, a stringed instrument very like a guitar. Mother sometimes could be coaxed to sing, and the younger children seldom tired of listening to them.

Parlor games, including guessing games such as charades, kept the family together and occupied during the winter. Edwin was the star in this game and was never modest about taking a bow.

During the school year, the children often gathered around a large table in the study to do their homework. Even though there was a big difference in their ages, it was expected that everyone would spend the time to their advantage and be ready to help a younger sibling. Edwin admitted that this family discipline prepared him for much of the concentrated study later in his career.

Edwin loved to read. Adventure books were his favorites, particularly novels by Jules Verne that dealt with fantasies of the future and other worlds. Another favorite was H. Rider Haggard's *King Solomon's Mines*. The one subject in school he never mastered was spelling, a fault that shows up even in his professional papers later in life.

INTRODUCTION TO THE STARS

The first inkling that Edwin might want to study stars in the heavens came about when he was visiting his mother's family. His maternal grandfather, William Henderson James, had rigged up a small telescope in his backyard. Edwin was fascinated. He spent the better part of early summer nights staring through the magic glass. In November, at the time of his eighth birthday, Edwin was asked what he particularly wanted for a present that year. He replied that he wanted to stay up all night looking through the telescope. No one took him seriously. Surely the young scientist would fall asleep long before dawn. He might get sick in the cold November night, and what about school the following morning? Edwin promised to wrap up well and to make the school bell on time.

Edwin prepared carefully. He had a cap with earmuffs and a fuzzy gray sweater to keep him warm. In the pocket of his jacket he stuffed a gigantic sandwich and two cookies that he never remembered to finish. The clear sky was perfect for viewing. An arch of stars twinkled against an ink-washed background, and only a sliver of moon brightened the heavens. Early on, there was a stroke of light that Edwin thought must be a shooting star or maybe a comet, but Grandpa James, who would have known, had long ago gone to bed. Besides, Edwin wouldn't have dared to leave his telescope for fear he might miss something else lighting up the sky. Morning came too soon.

Grandpa James was the only one he talked to

about stars. When Edwin was twelve he wrote a letter to his grandfather discussing the possibilities that life might be found on Mars. Dr. James found it so interesting he sent it to a newspaper in Springfield, Missouri. It was published without fanfare, but later in Hubble's life the story was exaggerated in the retelling. It was eventually reported that he had written a scholarly paper on the subject. Not quite so, but he had used his imagination brilliantly, a trait that served him well when trying to unravel space mysteries as an astronomer.

When Edwin was fourteen he had an emergency appendectomy. Today it is a simple operation, but during Edwin's childhood, dangerous infections often set in, and bed rest was the prescription for recovery. This was all to his liking. He had plenty of time to read his books and be the center of attention for a worried family.

Books weren't his only passion. He was interested in sports. In the last year of high school he grew to his full height of 6 feet 2 inches (188 cm). He was a good basketball player, and he also won medals on the track team for his pole vaulting records. At home he played tennis with brothers and sisters on a court marked off in their backyard.

Schoolwork was easy for Edwin, much to the annoyance of his brother Bill, who studied much harder but couldn't match Edwin's grades. Edwin graduated from high school in 1906. During the

*Edwin (right) with his sister Lucy (second from right)
and brother William (third from right)*

graduation ceremony the principal made the following remark: "Edwin Hubble, I have watched
you for four years and I have never seen you study
for ten minutes." After a long pause he continued,
"But I hereby present you with a scholarship to
the University of Chicago."

There was laughter and applause, and Edwin
accepted the honor with a bow to the audience and
a grin on his face. He was a show-off to some, an
admired example to others, yet he was never
accused of modesty.

CHAPTER THREE

COLLEGE AT LAST

Edwin entered college at the early age of sixteen. Although younger than many in his chosen field of astronomy, he had an air of authority. Some called it swagger. It was the first time Edwin was on his own, and he liked the feeling of independence. His father, however, still exercised authority from a distance.

BOXING DAYS

Because of Edwin's size, Alonzo Stagg, the university's football coach, tried to recruit him to try out for the team. Stagg happened to make the suggestion in front of Edwin's father, who was visiting for the weekend. Much to Edwin's embarrassment, John Hubble immediately vetoed the idea. Football was a violent sport to be avoided, he reasoned. Why not try out for baseball?

It seemed an unfair ruling, so Edwin immediately started collecting statistics on baseball injuries, hoping Father would realize football would be safer. Despite Edwin's efforts, or perhaps because of them, John Hubble decided to make the rules even stricter. Team sports were too rough and took far too much time from important academic pursuits. He insisted that Edwin make a solemn promise not to join any team or even practice with a squad.

Edwin followed instructions to the letter, forgetting to mention to his family that he had taken up boxing. He was not only good; he was great. His coach suggested he turn professional. This was not Edwin's intention, but he secretly would have liked to surprise his father with a medal after winning a championship match. Instead it was a buried family secret until much later, after his father's death, when he bragged about his matches. Sister Lucy remembers Edwin's bitterness about his father's interference in his life, but the rift was not deep enough to fracture family unity, and Edwin managed to do pretty much as he pleased while living in Chicago.

THE YERKES OBSERVATORY

Edwin was particularly interested in mathematics and astronomy. The University of Chicago had one of the finest observatories in the country, the Yerkes Observatory, which housed an enormous 40-inch (102-cm) refractor telescope. When the instrument was dedicated in 1897, it was the largest refractor telescope in the world. It is still the largest today. The massive lenses in very large refractor telescopes tend to flex under their own weight, causing them to distort images. All major telescopes of this size or larger now use not a lens but a concave mirror to focus light. Unlike a lens that one must see through, a mirror can be supported from behind without blocking light, minimizing distortion due to gravity.

When Hubble entered the University of Chicago, George Ellery Hale, a pioneer in astrophysical research, was the head of the astronomy department. The great refractor telescope came to the university almost by accident.

Hale learned that the University of Southern California planned to build the world's largest telescope, using glass disks cast by a company in Paris, France, to be polished into a 40-inch (102-cm) lens by glass finishers in Cambridgeport, Massachusetts. When the University of Southern California was forced to abandon the project because of lack of funds, Hale stepped forward and urged the University of Chicago to acquire the half-completed lens.

There was still the job of raising money to

The Yerkes Observatory

construct the telescope, and of course there had to be a building to house the delicate, but huge, instrument. Hale proved to be a master salesman as well as scientist. At his urging the funding was provided by transit tycoon Charles Tyson Yerkes. The next problem was where to locate the observatory. Hale stipulated that it had to be away from city lights and the smog of heavy industry. Yet it should be within 100 miles (161 km) of the university campus and easily accessible. Another benefactor came forward and gave the university a 53-acre (21-hectare) tract of land ½ mile (0.8 km) north of Geneva Lake in Wisconsin, about 80 miles (129 km) northwest of Chicago. The property was surrounded by the beautiful summer homes of Chicago's elite.

The building to house the large telescope required a dome 90 feet (27 m) high. The architect, Henry Ives Cobb, was fond of ornamentation, and for the Yerkes Observatory he let his imagination run wild. Everywhere in the structure, on stone columns and arched windows, there are hundreds of carved animals and fanciful signs of the zodiac. It looks like a medieval castle.

When Hubble first saw the building, he confessed to a friend that it was a silly monstrosity. He felt that the frills were a waste of money, but when he realized that funds had not been stinted on the practical design of working equipment, his criticism turned to praise. The entire floor of the observatory was electrically controlled just like an elevator. When he stepped onto the floor and pushed a button, the floor lifted him directly to the instrument's eyepiece. He felt he was truly reaching toward heaven.

Hubble (back row, fifth from right) at the Yerkes Observatory

As on the night of his eighth birthday, he wanted to spend the entire night staring at the stars. His first impulse was to monopolize this chance to see the sky in such detail. Yet he soon found that every minute of precious time had to be allotted to a scientific project. This meant not randomly scanning the sky, but photographing it for a particular purpose. The original projects outlined by Hale called for the study of the sun during its many phases of emitting powerful bursts of energy. From the beginning, Hubble was fascinated with objects farther out in space, but this star gazing had to take place only after assignments.

The faculty at the time of Hubble's study included the eminent astronomer Forrest Moulton and the famous physicists Albert Michelson and Robert Millikan. Hubble couldn't have come to the university at a better time. He worked for a while as assistant in Millikan's laboratory. Millikan remembered Hubble as a bright young man enchanted with the mysteries of the sky, but who could concentrate just as hard on a game of tennis or designing ways to pull pranks on unsuspecting classmates. On one occasion, Hubble threw raw eggs out of his window at the somberly clad theology students who shared the same dorm in Chicago.

STUDYING ABROAD

For Hubble, the four years at the university slipped by in a hurry. He was still young. He hadn't fathomed a way to earn a living in mathematics and astronomy. When one of his professors suggested he might want to teach these subjects, he answered, "That would tie me down." Yet he enjoyed academic life. He hoped to win a Rhodes scholarship, which would permit him to study at a university in England. This would be an impressive addition to his résumé for almost any career.

The scholarship is awarded each year to an unmarried student between nineteen and twenty-five years of age who shows a superior academic record, excels in sports, and displays fine character traits. Edwin's sophomoric pranks were overlooked, and in September 1910 he received word that he had been selected to receive the honor. It was a two-year scholarship, later extended to three in Edwin's case. This included all his living expenses and a modest sum for spending money. Now he was truly on his own.

Instead of asking to be assigned to Cambridge University where he could have taken advanced courses in science and mathematics, he reported to Oxford University's Queen's College, where he was to study law. This pleased his father immensely, but Edwin later said that his family had not influenced his decision. He really didn't have a definite goal. He still considered his love of astronomy as simply an interesting hobby that wouldn't quite pay the bills for the sort of life he was used to. He'd have to find another way to earn a living, and law might be the answer.

His days at Oxford were to have a lasting influence on his life. Edwin was impressed by those in the spotlight, whether they achieved center stage for academic accomplishments, diplomatic credentials, or theatrical renown. It was as if he hoped some of the fame would tilt his way. Oxford was a meeting place for the famous, and Edwin went out of his way to meet them. Some thought of him as a snob, but a good-natured one.

Hubble particularly admired the British way of life. He courted their style, which he felt matched their reserved, dignified behavior. He started to dress in plus fours, a style of knickers popular at the time, topped with tweed jackets with leather buttons. He often covered his carefully combed head of hair with a huge cap, and he sported a cane. Edwin even mimicked British speech with a smattering of "by Joves," and he returned home with a British accent that he kept throughout his life. He took to smoking a pipe, which he clenched between his teeth whether it was lit or not. He was rarely without it. He acquired the habit to make himself look older and wiser, he later remembered. Although impressively tall, he was still barely out of his teens. England polished the raw look of youth.

He learned the superficial rules of behavior, enjoying all things British, even their sports: boating and rowing and cricket. He admired their

While at Oxford, Hubble absorbed many elements of English culture, including wearing knickers.

centuries of history. At this time in his life he started a very impressive book collection. Two of his first acquisitions were a sixteenth-century Latin book of verse and a volume of works by Thomas Robert Malthus. The books may have been purchases made only to impress his friends, but considering Hubble's eclectic tastes later in life, it is probable they were read and enjoyed.

He also wanted to learn more about the cultures of Europe. During two summers he traveled 2,000 miles (3,219 km) in Germany, mostly by bicycle. There were other quick trips through the French countryside and one guided tour through Switzerland. During his visit to each country, Hubble absorbed a bit of the culture. He still loved America and would share his views of patriotism with whoever would listen, but he was learning that the world was a much bigger place than what he had known in Missouri and even in the heady circles of the University of Chicago.

CHAPTER FOUR

A CAREER DECISION

He returned home with a bachelor's degree in law, and here the history of Edwin Hubble is clouded. It has been said that he practiced law in Kentucky for a year before returning to the University of Chicago. There are no records, however, of his having been admitted to the bar to practice law in that state. Instead, one source states that he taught school and was hired to translate certain documents from German into English.

As a vacation job, he signed on with a group of land surveyors to map the route of a railway line in northern Wisconsin—not particularly the sort of work suited for a returning Oxford scholar. It is as if Edwin were trying to sample different lifestyles before settling on a career.

Northern Wisconsin was a wilderness region at the time, supporting only a few lumber camps, long before tourists had staked a claim on this land of lakes. On one occasion when Hubble was hiking alone, he was surprised and attacked by two men. One heavyset lumberjack grappled him from behind, trying to pin his arms at his sides, while the other started tearing at his jacket pocket to steal what money he might be carrying. Hubble half spun on his heel, freeing his hands. As the first man stepped backward, Hubble landed a full blow to his face, knocking him unconscious. The second thief was last seen sprinting through the forest. Hubble's college boxing days had not been wasted.

When the season ended, the work crew gathered at the railroad station to return to Chicago only to be told that no train was due for a week. The surveyors decided not to wait but set out on foot for the nearest town. For three days they were without food. The danger and hardships of that experience mounted with each retelling. Edwin was never a dull conversationalist and never bashful about giving his stories a hero's edge.

BACK TO CHICAGO

Still Hubble wasn't sure what he wanted to do with his life. He was attracted to the field of astronomy, but to abandon his law training seemed wasteful. His father, of course, assumed that Edwin would join a law firm either in Illinois or Missouri. Without consulting his family, Edwin wrote a letter in the spring of 1914 to Forest Ray Moulton, the astronomy professor at the University of Chicago, to ask about the possibility of returning as a graduate student. Moulton enthusiastically recommended him to Edwin R. Frost, the current director of Yerkes Observatory, where all the graduate work would take place.

Frost gladly accepted Hubble as a pupil and arranged for him to receive a scholarship that included both tuition and living expenses. Hubble was delighted. He had not wanted to ask his family for funds when his father did not support his choice of careers, but Edwin was later to say that he knew that "even if I were second-rate or third-rate, it is astronomy that matters." By the time his father knew of his decision, arrangements had been made and argument was futile.

"Even if I were second-rate or third-rate, it is astronomy that matters."

Before starting his graduate work, Hubble received an invitation to accompany Professor Frost to a meeting of the American Astronomical Society, which was to take place at Northwestern University in Evanston, Illinois, in August of 1914. Frost urged Edwin to come immediately, "for it will well be worthwhile for your future work."

Hubble was introduced to many prestigious

astronomers of the day. He was elected a member of the society that year, a fine tribute to a novice scientist. It was at this meeting that Hubble heard Dr. Vesto M. Slipher from Lowell Observatory read a paper describing his research studying mysterious objects in the farthest reaches of outer space. These remote objects were called nebulae.

The term *nebula,* which is Latin for "cloud," was used to designate various faint cloudy objects that, unlike comets, appear to be stationary when viewed from Earth. No one had been able to define just what these objects were. They might be either a mass of luminous gas or groups of very faint stars far away from our solar system.

At the 1914 meeting Slipher showed the first well-exposed photographs of the spectra of spiral nebulae—nebulae that are spiral shaped. Slipher had determined the speed and direction in which thirteen nebulae were moving through space. The measurements were quite unexpected. In contrast to the stars previously measured, many nebulae were receding at unbelievable speeds. Most astronomers of the day refused to believe the figures presented, calling them inaccurate numbers created by sloppy research. It was a puzzle that fired Hubble's imagination and sent him on a search that would keep him busy his entire career.

When Hubble began studying astronomy, scientists knew little about the cloudlike nebulae that faintly appeared through their telescopes. Pictured here is the nebula America in the constellation Swan.

GALAXIES FAR, FAR AWAY?

Hubble began his research on a smaller telescope in Yerkes Observatory. He chose the 24-inch (61-cm) reflector telescope, located beside the huge 40-inch (102-cm) telescope, simply because more time had been allotted to him on this one. (The larger telescope was principally reserved for solar observation.) Hubble attempted to photograph remote stars that seemed to be moving away from Earth. He compared his plates with those made by his colleagues approximately ten years earlier. Carefully examining the exposed photographic plates he produced, Hubble discovered twelve unknown variable stars—stars whose light varies on a regular pattern.

He wrote, "So far as I am aware, these are the faintest stars in which any appreciable motion has been found."

"So far as I am aware, these are the faintest stars in which any appreciable motion has been found."

He later proved that these faint stars were located far from the pull of our own solar system, but he was not ready to make such a claim as yet. He had heard what others had said about Slipher's research. He wanted to make absolutely sure that no one would ridicule his findings. He was meticulous in his research. One of his fellow astronomers described Hubble as an extraordinarily exact and careful scientist who normally refrained from making assertions that were not well supported by evidence, evidence that he himself questioned until he had exhausted all other explanations. Even in his early work, he exhibited patience combined with a creative talent that let him think ahead for explanations of the mysteries that continued to unfold before his eyes. He would first guess at the meaning of what he was seeing and then set about proving his guesswork.

His doctoral dissertation was entitled *Photographic Investigations of Faint Nebulae*. It was a relatively new field of research, although about two thousand nebulae had been found by this time. Most nebulae looked quite similar. They could not be pinpointed as stars. They looked like clouds against the night sky. Their origin and makeup depended on just how far away they were from Earth. If, as Hubble supposed, they were in distant space, they might be clusters of galaxies. If they were within our own system, "their nature becomes a mystery."

"The spirals are stellar systems at distances to be measured in millions of years."

He wrote in his own journal that "the spirals are stellar systems at distances to be measured in millions of years," but it was some years before he was willing to publish his theory.

CHAPTER FIVE

OFF TO WAR

By the spring of 1917, a war had been raging in Europe for three years. The United States had been able to stay out of the war, but on April 6 President Woodrow Wilson pledged his support to the British Allies. Even before there was a military draft, young men were signing up for service overseas. Universities were emptying fast.

Meanwhile, Hubble had been monitoring the completion of the 100-inch (254-cm) mirror to be installed on the new telescope at the Mount Wilson Observatory in California. The observatory director was George Ellery Hale, the same man who had masterminded the installation at Yerkes. He remembered Hubble from undergraduate days.

Hale sent a letter to Hubble inviting him to join the staff in what everyone agreed would be one of the most exciting periods in astronomical research. The largest telescope in the world would soon be operational. Who would be the first to analyze the results of this glimpse into deep space?

A SURPRISING DECISION

Hubble was just finishing his doctoral thesis. It was a tremendous opportunity and a flattering one at that. He had yet to make his mark on the scientific world, but after much deliberation he sent Hale his answer by telegram. "Regret I cannot accept your invitation. I am off to war."

It was a surprise to his family and his coworkers. He was twenty-eight years old, and his life's work was just beginning, yet it could not have been a rash decision. As he said later, "I never considered I had a choice."

During the three years he had spent in England and on subsequent trips to continental Europe, Hubble had made many friends. The news that familiar places were being devastated by artillery and that peace-loving people were being forced to take up arms made the decision to join the Allied force an easy one.

He felt a duty, and he acted upon it, yet he did not go to kill "the Huns," as Germans were bitterly called. Hubble had spent much time in Germany and admired the people he met, which heightened his exasperation with the aggressive

Hubble's military ID

tactics Kaiser Wilhelm II was using on the inno-
cent population. He lectured everyone who would
listen about the unfairness of placing blanket
blame on the German population for the horrors
of war. Hubble was very emotional about the subject. Most of his friends were quite willing to
damn all Germans. He was going to war to bring
about a quick peace, to stop the killing, he said.

Hubble stayed up all night to finish his doctoral thesis, and the following morning, after
making his oral defense of the thesis, he joined
the army. Hubble was not alone in his decision.
Thirty-four young men who had just graduated

from the University of Chicago joined the service that spring.

Hubble was first sent to Officers Training Camp at Fort Sheridan, Illinois. Classes took place from morning to night—nothing new to him—but this was an entirely different field from science and law. He discovered he admired military order and discipline.

MILITARY SUCCESS

With his exceptional academic background and his natural sense of leadership, it was not long before Hubble was given the rank of captain and put in charge of training new recruits from Illinois and Wisconsin. On August 5, 1917, the 85th Black Hawk Division was formed. Its emblem was a black hawk on a three-cornered red shield. In late August, more promotions followed. Captain Hubble was made commander of the 2nd Battalion of the 343rd Infantry. In December he was promoted to major. His letters home convey the pride he took in his advancement.

Hubble immediately took to military life. Pictures show him standing stiffly at attention even in family photos. He was an imposing figure in his uniform, 6 foot 2 inches (188 cm), ramrod straight. With Edwin's encouragement, sister Lucy joined ranks and served as a nurse's aide during World War I.

*Hubble stands at attention beside his sister Lucy,
a nurse's aide.*

Hubble could see that the military had a practical, efficient way of getting things done. Orders were given, no questions asked. But there were times when he was not an admirer of some of the nonsensical requirements of army drill.

Hubble was riding his bicycle on the drill grounds one day when he saw a general approach. He stopped, saluted, and said, "Good morning, General. Nice day, sir."

The general stopped to give Hubble a lecture on proper protocol. He ordered Hubble to state his rank and name and what he was doing. Hubble followed the instructions to the letter. He saluted the general and reported, "Sir, Major Hubble, 383rd Infantry, is getting on his bicycle and riding away."

The story was repeated by some who had observed the exchange, and they started calling him the "Riding Away Major." The incident helped break down Hubble's own image of being a no-nonsense officer.

American troops were pouring into Europe as fast as they could be trained. Hubble's unit finally boarded troop ships on September 8, 1918. German submarines had taken a heavy toll on transatlantic shipping in the early days of the war, but by 1918 the danger had decreased. Convoys were guarded by warships, and airplanes and observation balloons helped spot submarines.

Hubble's unit landed at Liverpool, England, but was immediately transferred to other ships to take them to the French port of Cherbourg. From there the Black Hawk Division moved south toward Bordeaux.

Later stories about Hubble's war effort indicate that he was wounded in combat. Records, however, show that his division had arrived too late to get to the battlefront. A more reliable source tells that Hubble did receive an injury during his tour of duty, a broken arm caused by the accidental explosion of a grenade. Hubble never spoke of it, and it seems that this may just have been a story by others to make him more a hero.

Within six weeks of the time Hubble landed on foreign soil, the war was over. Still, it took a long, complicated process to get many American troops home. Because of his legal education, Hubble was transferred to the courtmartial branch of the army, and before returning home he was appointed administrator of a group of American officers admitted to the universities of Oxford, Cambridge, and Wales for short courses.

Hubble returned to the States in August 1919. He was mustered out in San Francisco and traveled straight to Pasadena, California, to see if Hale's original offer to work at the Mount Wilson Observatory was still valid. The answer was an enthusiastic yes.

CHAPTER SIX

MAPPING THE SKY

The telescope at the Mount Wilson Observatory was the finest, most powerful in the world, and George Ellery Hale knew just how he wanted it used. He brought Hubble on board knowing he had always been primarily interested in the far reaches of space. For once they'd have an opportunity to probe deeper than ever before. Both Hale and Hubble respected each other's qualities. Hubble was known as a painstaking researcher, Hale as a brilliant astronomer with a proven ability to attract funds to finance exciting projects.

Since his days at the Yerkes Observatory, Hale's interest had shifted from the sun to spiral nebulae. The Hooker Telescope at Mount Wilson, named after the wealthy donor who gave funds for the glass disk that became its mirror, would help them unravel the mysteries of the nebulae.

STUDYING THE NEBULAE

In Hubble's studies of nebulae, it became evident to him that some of these regions were great clouds of dust and gas lit from within by young stars that were just beginning to form. Hubble was interested in accurately measuring the distances to particular spiral nebulae. He also wondered if these nebulae were stationary or moving relative to Earth.

Hubble's objective was to study the nebulae known to be within our own galaxy and compare them with objects he guessed were millions of light-years farther away from us. Hubble first used several wide-angle cameras attached to an instrument called an astrograph to photograph a large area of the night sky. He could then zero in on the more interesting, more puzzling objects that seemed to follow no rules set out in previous textbooks.

Hubble was very meticulous with his classification of all nebulae he studied. Just one night's sighting was not considered enough. Only after a series of accurate observations would the information be entered in his log.

Many years later, Hubble's colleague N. U. Mayall wrote, "His knowledge of individual nebulae was encyclopedic. He knew literally hundreds of objects in sufficient detail to recall their structure and their relationship to neighboring ones. He knew the Milky Way as thoroughly as any port pilot threading his way through a system of channels, bars, and buoys."

Another coworker remembers that Hubble entered the dome of the observatory one night when a young student from Berkeley was trying unsuccessfully to find an object. Without leaving the floor to reach the eyepiece of the telescope, he called out the exact location. "The declination is plus five degrees."

To gain such an accurate vision of the heavens, he had to spend hours in lonely concentration. Hubble knew that an astronomer's life is apt to be divided into segments due to the whims of nature. Cloud patterns and the phases of the moon that lighten and darken the sky dictate when close observation is possible. Although Mount Wilson had been carefully selected as having the best chance of clear weather, there were only a few nights every month when conditions were perfect.

Everyone hoped for clear nights. Warm days

"He knew the Milky Way as thoroughly as any port pilot threading his way through a system of channels, bars, and buoys."
—N. U. Mayall

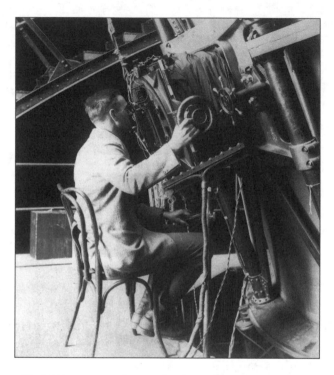

*Hubble gazes through the Hooker Telescope
at Mount Wilson.*

were a catastrophe. If the glass mirror was as few
as 10 degrees (5.6° C) warmer than the night air,
it would take twenty-four hours for the mirror to
cool, and the telescope would be useless during
that time. Thick glass does not cool evenly. Heat
on the surface of the glass dissipates first so that
the outside of the mirror becomes cooler than the
core of the mirror. The temperature difference
within the mirror causes it to warp temporarily.

Consequently, images viewed through the telescope become distorted. To help solve the problem for the Mount Wilson telescope, a system of coils carrying cold water was installed on the back of the disk. The astronomers had to guess what the night temperature would be so that they could keep the mirror at that temperature during the day.

The phases of the moon limited some observation. A bright moon obscured the faint light coming from objects far away. During periods when Hubble could not use the telescope, he turned his work schedule from night to day and studied photographic plates that had been processed before.

LIFE AT THE OBSERVATORY

When the observatory at Mount Wilson first opened, astronomers had to rough it by camping out in a small one-story cabin that housed their library and living quarters. By the time Hubble arrived, this building had been enlarged, so that when an astronomer was on a "run," as his block of time was called, he could sleep close by in relative comfort. The road to the mountain was much improved, and the commute to the observatory from the town of Pasadena was cut to a mere two hours by car. More extensive offices in Pasadena, at 813 Santa Barbara Street, were also provided.

Hubble worked on all instruments available—the 60-inch (152-cm) and the 100-inch (254-

cm) reflector telescopes and the 10-inch (25-cm) astrograph. At one time it was noted that he spent nineteen hours without a break photographing one area in the Ophiuchus galaxy. For three nights he repeated the process to note any changes.

Many years later, one of the scientists with whom he worked, Dr. Osterbrook, admitted that Hubble's photographic plates sometimes tended to be less clear than those created by the other astronomers, but he had creative insight that allowed him to guess what the photos were showing, and then make more observations to prove his guesses true.

One of the reasons his early plates were not always clear was his refusal to break off photographing the sky when conditions were not perfect. Being one of the newer members of the staff, he had to share the perfect viewing time with others. Hubble was often thought to be aloof and rather unfriendly by his professional coworkers. Yet this was not the picture others had of him. He worked hard, but he also knew how to relax.

An avid fisherman, Hubble often took off for the wilderness of Colorado. He admitted that some of his best thinking was done while casting for an elusive trout in a clear, rushing stream.

But Hubble found that the most relaxing activity after a busy schedule at the observatory was spending time with the young woman who was to become his wife.

CHAPTER SEVEN

SHARING A LIFE

Grace Burke Leib first met Hubble in 1920 when she accompanied William H. Wright and his wife, Elna, to visit Mount Wilson. Wright was a well-known astronomer himself, who worked at the Lick Observatory, also in California. Wright, who was considerably older than Hubble, told Grace, "He is a hard worker. He wants to find out everything about the universe. That shows how young he is."

This did not discourage her at all. She was much impressed by Hubble's commanding presence, and she was truly intrigued by his explanation of his work. Hubble spoke of his research as a dream and an adventure. His enthusiasm easily spread to her.

However, Grace was married at the time to Earl Warren Leib, a mining engineer, whom she had known in college. A year after that first trip to Mount Wilson, her husband was killed in an abandoned mine he was examining. It was a shocking blow, but her parents and friends helped ease her loneliness. She moved back to her family home.

FALLING IN LOVE

During the next two years, Grace and Edwin saw each other infrequently, but each encounter made a lasting impression on Grace. Her diary records even the briefest meeting. Years later she recalled her first impression of Edwin Hubble as "an Olympian, tall, strong, and beautiful, with the shoulders of the Hermes of Praxiteles, and with benign serenity."

Such hero worship was to continue during her entire life. We don't have Edwin's words on the subject of his bride-to-be, but his sister Betsy said that "he was quite smitten. Edwin had had only one love in his youth, but the young woman broke off their engagement because she knew she could never substitute for Mars, the nebulae, and such."

None of Hubble's friends at the time remember his ever acting as a rejected suitor. As master of his own fate, he probably waited for the right moment in his career to take on added responsibilities.

Grace was a beautiful, almost fragile, young woman. In contrast to Edwin's tall military bearing, she stood barely as tall as his shoulder. Yet she was active in sports, loved horseback riding, swimming, and hiking. She graduated from Stanford University, earning the honored Phi Beta Kappa award for excellent scholarship. She was also an officer in the collegiate sorority Alpha Phi.

It was not until 1923 that Hubble started to call on Grace regularly. When he found she loved hiking, he planned extensive walking tours through some of the most difficult terrain the Sierra Nevada mountain range of California had to offer, often shouldering a heavy pack that con-

Edwin and Grace sit in front of the Burke family house on their wedding day.

tained books as well as food. Grace loved this time together; they could finally get to know each other.

It was not long before their engagement was announced. The wedding took place on the morning of February 26, 1924. The service was performed by the Burke's family priest. Edwin's family did not attend. It is not clear whether they were even invited. Only Grace's parents and her sister witnessed the ceremony.

After a wedding breakfast, the couple drove north to a cottage owned by the Burke family at Pebble Beach. Grace wrote in her diary that they cooked their first meal over a bonfire on the beach. When they returned to Pasadena, they packed their bags for an extended trip to Europe, where Edwin was able to show his bride many of the favorite spots he had discovered during his college days.

APPOINTMENT WITH FAME

They returned to a rented home in Pasadena and planned to resume a normal private life. That was not to be. On November 24, 1924, Hubble's name reached the headlines. The public read an astonishing article in the *New York Times* that quoted Hubble as having found proof that spiral nebulae were indeed galaxies in their own right, so remote that the light by which they were currently seen had left its source long before humans lived on Earth.

The headlines read, "Finds Spiral Nebulae are Stellar Systems. Doctor Hubbell Confirms View they are 'Island Universes.'" Only the spelling of Hubble's name was incorrect.

"Finds Spiral Nebulae are Stellar Systems. Doctor Hubbell Confirms View they are 'Island Universes.'"
—*New York Times*, November 24, 1924

The article continued. "The number of spiral nebulae the observatory officials have reported to the institution is very great, amounting to hundreds of thousands, and their apparent sizes range from small objects, almost star-like in character, to the great nebula in Andromeda, which stretches across an angle of some 3 degrees in the heavens, about six times the diameter of the full moon as seen from Earth."

Suddenly Hubble was the man of the hour. He found his time taken up by newspaper reporters and by scientists all over the world asking for more information, more proof of such outrageous findings. Not everyone agreed with Hubble's figures. Adriaan van Maanen had spent twelve years studying the movement of the spiral nebulae within his range of observation. He concluded

Hubble poses with a photo of the Andromeda galaxy.

that if they were as far removed as Hubble stated, the velocity of their movement would exceed the speed of light, which is impossible.

Both men were respected scientists. The administration of the Mount Wilson Observatory and the California Institute of Technology wanted no part in a public dispute, but words became heated and scientists started to take sides. Maanen was a close friend of Hale, the director of the Mount Wilson Observatory. Maanen was sociable.

People liked him. Among his peers, Hubble always seemed elusive, distant. Some thought he had a giant ego that bruised easily, while others who claimed to know him personally vowed he was easygoing and articulate, never brusque. There was rarely a moderate assessment of Hubble's personality.

AWARDS AND RECOGNITION

Now that the press had a condensed report of his findings, Hubble submitted a professional paper about his theory at the prestigious gathering of the American Society for the Advancement of Science. At the meeting, a thousand-dollar prize would be given to the most notable scientific advancement of the year.

On January 1, 1925, Hubble's paper, titled "Cepheid Variables in Spiral Nebulae," was read to the convening group of scientists. Joel Stebbins, a friend of Hubble and the secretary of the American Astronomical Society, made sure the paper was submitted in the proper manner to the committee on prizes.

Stebbins enclosed a letter which stated, "The paper is the product of a young man of conspicuous and recognized ability in a field which he has made particularly his own. It opens up depths of space previously inaccessible to investigation and gives promise of still greater advances in the near future. Meanwhile, it has already expanded one hundred fold the known volume of the material universe and has apparently settled the long-mooted question of the nature of spirals, showing them to be agglomerations of stars almost comparable in extent with our own galaxy."

> "The paper is the product of a young man of conspicuous and recognized ability in a field which he has made particularly his own."
>
> —Joel Stebbins

On the thirteenth of February, *Science* magazine announced that the committee had decided to have two scientists share the prize, Dr. Edwin Hubble and Dr. L. R. Cleveland, specialist in termites. Although Hubble had to share the honor, his name appeared for the first time in *Who's Who in America* for 1924–25, and he finally had the backing of his peers, at least most of them.

UNIVERSAL ACCEPTANCE

It was not until ten years later, when two young astronomers took over the job of checking Maanen's data and found errors in his calculations, that Hubble's "island universe" theory was universally accepted. Adriaan van Maanen's research had depended on measuring almost imperceptible changes on photographic plates. The changes he was attempting to measure were at the very limits of the precision of his equipment. A dedicated scientist, Maanen found it hard to admit that the conclusions of his life's work would have to be altered so drastically. It is to his credit that he came to accept the newer figures.

With Hubble's new prominence in the field of astronomy, his workload increased, and during the first year of married life, Grace found she had to share her husband's time at home with his work on the mountain. On the days he was to start his "run" of observation, he would carefully pack his clothing, a tin of tobacco, some books, and a flashlight into a worn suitcase stenciled "Major Edwin P. Hubble." Then he was off to gather more information about what was happening in the far reaches of space no one had studied before.

CHAPTER EIGHT

HOW FAR TO THE STARS?

Hubble certainly wasn't the first one to dream of measuring distances between objects in space. For centuries, humans have been trying to calculate how far away the sun and moon and stars are from the earth. When Hubble began his research, however, most methods available to him were only useful for measuring distances to the closest stars. These methods proved inadequate for determining distances to the extremely remote objects that he was exploring.

Hubble's amazing calculations of distance in outer space would not have been possible without the painstaking work of Henrietta Swan Leavitt, a brilliant woman who worked on the staff of the Harvard Observatory. She was interested in measuring the brightness of stars from photographic plates.

CEPHEIDS

In 1908 she came across stars that showed a distinct variation of brightness, always on a regular pattern. She found a direct relationship between the length of time for a complete cycle of brightness to take place and the star's average luminosity—the average amount of light given off. In other words, she proved that any stars that have the same cycle, ten days for example, must also give off the same amount of light. Some stars completed their cycle of brightness every few hours. Most had longer cycles measured in days. These variable stars are called *Cepheids*.

Hubble took this information and went further to say that "the nature of the variability of Cepheids is identical throughout the universe." This meant that whenever a newfound Cepheid was located, if that star took the same amount of time to pass through its brightness cycle as did a Cepheid closer to Earth, that star must also give off the same amount of light as the Cepheid closer to Earth. This would remain true

> **"The nature of the variability of Cepheids is identical throughout the universe."**

even if the remote Cepheid were located in a distant galaxy.

As Hubble probed outer space as far as the Mount Wilson telescope could see, he discovered Cepheids in the distant nebulae. Because they were so far away, they appeared much fainter than nearby Cepheids with the same cycle. However, Hubble realized that the distant Cepheids only seemed fainter because they were farther away.

The apparent brightness of any object decreases in proportion to the square of its distance from the observer. Thus to make an object appear one ten-thousandth as bright, you must move it a hundred times farther away. By using this ratio to compare the apparent brightness of two Cepheids that are known to give off the same amount of light, Hubble could estimate the distance to the faint, remote Cepheids, and to the nebulae in which they were located. This was the key to settling the dispute over the nature of spiral nebulae.

Hubble carefully calculated the distance to the Cepheid variable stars in spiral nebulae. He could tell now that they were too far away to be part of our own Milky Way galaxy. He thus proved that the universe is made up of many distinct galaxies, a concept that radically changed the perception of the universe.

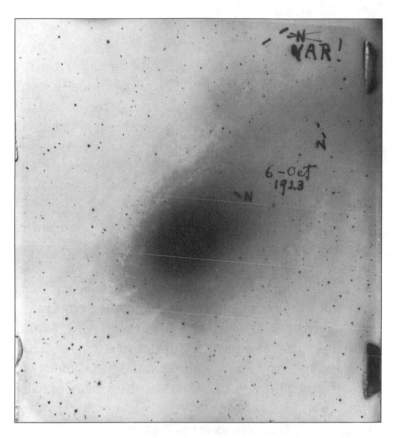

*In 1923, Hubble examined this image of the
Andromeda nebula and labeled three novae (stars
that suddenly increase in brightness) with an N.
To Hubble's excitement, one of these turned out to be a
Cepheid variable, and he relabeled the star "VAR!"
This Cepheid, and others later discovered, enabled
Hubble to determine that the Andromeda nebula is
in fact a galaxy separate from our own.*

HUBBLE CLASSIFICATION

Hubble developed other methods for determining the distances to galaxies. These methods depend on some assumptions about characteristics that galaxies have in common. For example, if two spiral galaxies appear to have the same shape, general appearance, and speed of rotation, he concluded that the two galaxies may be basically similar in size.

Suppose that when viewing these two spiral galaxies through the same telescope, one of these spiral galaxies covers ten times more area in the sky than another. Suppose also that the galaxy that looks bigger has one hundred times the apparent brightness of the other. Then, if we assume that the galaxies are much alike in terms of actual size and brightness, the conclusion follows that the fainter galaxy must be ten times more distant than the brighter one. This can be determined with two ratios. An increase in distance reduces any object's apparent size in direct proportion to the change in distance, so an object ten times as far away as an object of equal size would appear ten times as small. Also, an object ten times as far away as an object with the same original brightness would appear only one hundredth as bright. Both these relationships support the idea that the galaxies, despite their apparent differences in size and brightness, are actually quite similar in both respects. The apparent differences are caused by their distances from Earth.

Using these principles, if we know that the distance to one spiral galaxy, such as the Andromeda galaxy, is 2 million light-years away, we can then estimate the distance to the next similar spiral galaxy, which turns out to be 20 million light-years away. We can build on our approximations to calculate the distances to increasingly remote galaxies. This is called the *Pyramid of Distances*. This does not mean that exact distances can be proved. No two galaxies are exactly identical, and as the pyramid grows, there is a chance of multiplying errors. But Hubble's estimates were good enough to give a general picture of a broad universe filled with clusters of galaxies. To this day, his careful work in comparing the traits of the galaxies he was studying is known as the Hubble Classification.

MOTION OF GALAXIES

Hubble next attempted to determine the motion of the galaxies relative to each other. Surprisingly it is much easier to clock their motion, at least toward or away from us, than their distance from Earth.

The light from a star can be analyzed by viewing it with a spectroscope, an instrument that

The Andromeda galaxy is the galaxy
nearest to our own.

uses a prism to break up the light into the colors
of the visible spectrum: red, orange, yellow, green,
blue, indigo, and violet. This instrument operates
on the same principle that causes "white" sunlight
to separate into the colors of the rainbow when it
passes through tiny raindrops.

When scientists view light through a spectroscope, they see a series of bright bands of color,
called spectral lines, at specific positions along
the visible spectrum. The pattern of the spectral

lines gives scientists information about the object's chemical makeup. For example, the light of a star made up primarily of hydrogen will show a pattern of spectral lines unique to hydrogen. Thus, the composition of stars millions of light-years away can be determined simply by examining the light they give off.

Hubble and his colleagues compared the spectra of light from stars in distant galaxies. They found that the patterns of spectral lines matched those of familiar elements, such as hydrogen, helium, and calcium. The position of the spectral lines, however, was shifted toward the red end of the spectrum. What was causing the patterns of spectral lines to shift in such a manner?

The answer lay in a phenomenon that practically everyone has experienced. As a car passes by, the sound it makes as it comes toward you is very different from the sound it makes once it has passed you by. As the car approaches, the pitch of the sound increases, and you hear a progressively higher sound. Once it has passed, the pitch decreases, and you hear a progressively lower sound. This is called the Doppler effect.

Moving light sources also display the Doppler effect. As a light source approaches, the light it gives off is shifted toward the violet end of the spectrum. As a light source recedes, its light is shifted toward the red end of the spectrum.

Hubble realized that the shift in the spectral

lines observed in light from stars in distant galaxies was a result of the Doppler effect. Because the spectral lines were always shifted toward the red end of the spectrum, Hubble could determine that the galaxies were moving away from us. This phenomenon is aptly named red shift.

Hubble calculated that some distant objects were receding at a tremendous speed—up to 90 percent of the speed of light. He also noted that the more distant the object, the faster the object was moving away. This relationship between distance and speed is called the Hubble constant. It suggests that the universe is expanding, and apparently at an ever increasing rate.

Hubble was a man recognized during his lifetime as being the head of his field of research, yet not all honors he sought came his way. He was a loner, not apt to consult with others on the management of the observatory or with the California Institute of Technology (Caltech), which oversaw the use of the great instrument at Mount Wilson. He was never appointed to head the observatory. Instead, he spread his "charm" elsewhere. He and his brilliant, witty wife, Grace, frequently entertained a star-studded group of friends from such diverse fields as Hollywood and the literary world.

CHAPTER NINE

A PUBLIC LIFE

In the spring of 1926, the Hubbles moved into the home they would consider their permanent residence for the rest of their lives. Edwin had discovered the site in San Marino, California, on one of his hikes before his marriage. A narrow road wound through a stand of giant oaks. The view was magnificent. Distant mountains bordered the horizon, and to the south one looked down across the Gabriel Valley.

The property lay directly on an earthquake fault, which did not bother Hubble at all. In fact, he was pleased to point it out to all visitors. His annual salary had now tripled to $4,300, an adequate amount in those days, but the house and furnishings were a gift from Grace's parents.

The style of the house mimicked a building they had seen in Italy during their honeymoon. Hubble's study was located at one end of a sunken

The Hubble's San Marino house

library. Recessed bookshelves displayed his collection of valuable leather-bound volumes. There was a small fireplace in this room, but Hubble preferred the wide hearth in the beamed living room, which was almost always banked with large logs cut on the property. When he returned from work, he would settle in his favorite chair and enjoy a cocktail before dinner, something his father would have surely disapproved of. His pipe stand stood close by.

Grace's room of choice was the second-floor bedroom where her own writing desk was frequently put to use. There were few other bedrooms in the house, although they had hoped to raise a family. A pregnancy ended in a miscarriage a year after their marriage. Edwin was on the mountain at the time, but a doctor was called immediately. Grace refused to send a message to her husband, feeling his work was too important to be interrupted. Besides, there was nothing he could do to help at the time. At age thirty-seven, Grace felt the risks were too great to try another pregnancy. Edwin agreed, saying they were enough of a family to satisfy his wishes.

SURROUNDED BY CELEBRITIES

Instead, their life revolved around Edwin's work and their frequent entertaining. This would have been a surprise to Hubble's professional colleagues who never received invitations. Hubble kept his social life quite apart from his academic life. Hubble loved to collect celebrities. He was well aware he was becoming one himself, but surrounding himself with notables in other fields who begged for visits to the great observatory was a boon to his ego. He delighted in showing them the wonders of his world. He was frequently asked to give tours of the observatory as a special favor to visiting dignitaries.

It was a heady cast of characters. Cole Porter and Igor Stravinsky of music fame were friends. Anita Loos, screenwriter and author of the best-selling novel *Gentlemen Prefer Blondes* brought along her friends from the theatrical world. Helen

Hayes, Gary Cooper, Douglas Fairbanks, and newcomer Walt Disney were introduced to the Hubbles. Edwin had also kept in contact with some of his British friends. Sir Hugh Seymour Walpole, novelist and collector of manuscripts, helped make suggestions for acquisitions Edwin later added to his own collection. British actor George Arliss came to the mountain to see the amazing "gadget" that let him peer at the stars.

Hubble (middle) enjoyed the company of celebrities including Walt Disney (left) and British zoologist Julian Huxley (right).

Even Sir Anthony Eden, who was to become prime minister of England, came seeking a visit with "the man who knew the heavens as well as his home town."

Perhaps the most distinguished guest entertained by the entire faculty and staff at the observatory was Albert Einstein and his wife,

> "The man who knew the heavens as well as his home town."
> —Sir Anthony Eden

Elsa. According to biographer Robert W. Clark, fifty reporters and fifty photographers mobbed the poor man asking him "to define the fourth dimension in one word, state his theory of relativity in one sentence, give his views of prohibition, comment on politics and religion, and discuss the virtues of his violin."

No wonder Einstein, whose grasp of the English language was a bit shaky, tried to escape the crowd. Yet he had come expressly to see the instruments that were helping to prove some of his own theories about the structure of the universe. Europe had nothing like this. When Elsa Einstein, who was always at her husband's side, was told that the giant Hooker telescope was the instrument that had done much to help astronomers determine the structure of the universe, her reply was, "Well, well, my husband does that on the back of an old envelope."

Hubble had to share much of the glory of the

*Left to right: Milton L. Humason, observatory
technician; Hubble; Charles E. St. John, solar
astronomer; Albert A. Michelson, physicist; Albert
Einstein, physicist; William W. Campbell, president of
the University of California; and Walter S. Adams,
director of the Mount Wilson Observatory. This photo
was taken in the Mount Wilson Library during
Einstein's 1931 visit to the observatory.*

visit. An elderly Albert Michelson, who had made
the most exacting measurements of the speed of
light, was introduced to Einstein. This measure-
ment was one of the most important constants in
Einstein's theory of relativity, limiting velocity in

the physical world. At last many of the "fanciful" theories Einstein had put forth earlier in the century were being proved by practical application.

A formal dinner for Einstein was held at the Athenium, the Caltech faculty club. Everyone wanted to be invited, but fewer than three hundred people attended the formal affair. Einstein's translated speech was delivered by a Caltech professor, and Hubble's work on red shifts was singled out for honor.

A day or two later the Einsteins were invited to dine with Edwin and Grace at their home. Technical conversation was interspersed with talk about favorite books and the state of world politics. Einstein did not yet consider Hitler a threat. When Einstein was in a smaller group, he got along quite well in his broken English, sometimes reverting to French if he couldn't find the right words to translate his native German. With the Hubbles he felt comfortable.

On his second trip to Pasadena, Grace was asked to be his unofficial hostess, and she drove him to seminars and conferences. A warm camaraderie evolved.

"Your husband's work is beautiful—and—he has a beautiful spirit."
—Albert Einstein

One day he confided to Grace, "Your husband's work is beautiful—and—he has a beautiful spirit."

CHAPTER TEN

AT WAR AGAIN

Edwin Hubble's popularity in academic circles led to requests for lectures on both sides of the Atlantic. Although the money offered was modest, transportation and lavish accommodations were included. While in London they stayed in elaborately furnished quarters with service provided by a butler and maid. Grace wrote in one of her letters to her mother, "I believe that the first step in European civilization was taken when Homo Sapiens discovered that it was easier to coerce a weaker, not so intelligent H.S. to wait on him, than to invent labor-saving devices himself."

This shows Grace's sense of humor, but it also hints at the type of aristocratic political feelings both Edwin and Grace held. On one occasion Edwin expressed the opinion that civilization was divided between the common and boorish and the aristocratic and educated. Franklin Roosevelt was by far too liberal a president in their view.

Grace and Edwin Hubble frequently traveled overseas. Here, the couple stands on the deck of an ocean liner bound for England in 1936.

Hubble was receiving a lot of criticism for his time away from the observatory. Walter Adams, director of Mount Wilson, sent several letters of censure reminding Hubble that without the backing of the prestigious organization he represented, the trips would not be possible. The letters maintained that it was unfair to many of the other members of the staff that preference was being given to Hubble's travel plans.

A book Hubble had written, *The Realm of the Nebulae,* had become a classic, and he felt that his own stature as a leading astronomer justifiably added to the reputation of Mount Wilson. His lectures were good advertising. Only to Milton Humason, his closest associate on the mountain, did he admit that he feared that until the new giant 200-inch (508-cm) telescope that was being planned for nearby Mount Palomar was in operation, they had stretched their research as far into outer space as was possible. His days of making grandiose new discoveries were limited. He had to be content to reexamine figures and photographic plates already taken with the Mount Wilson telescope he had used so well in the past.

TRUSTED TECHNICIAN

Humason, one of Hubble's most admired helpers, was a man of little formal education. Yet he had trained himself to take accurate pictures of the points of reference Hubble was trying to map. It was he who produced many of the photographic plates showing the red shift of stars that proved Hubble's theory of galaxies rushing away from each other.

While still a teen, Humason had been a mule driver for the pack trains carrying supplies up the steep trail to Mount Wilson while the outbuildings for the observatory staff were being built. His next job on the mountain was janitor for the observatory. He was fascinated by what was going on around him. One of the junior astronomers taught him how to take plates of variable stars with the smaller cameras. He learned his lessons well. By the late 1920s he was recognized as an expert technician. Even Hubble relied on the accuracy and clarity of his work. While Hubble was out of the country, he often assigned Humason the job of furthering their combined research. Humason's earthy humor contrasted with Hubble's formal reserve. But Hubble, despite his aristocratic ideas, could appreciate how far Humason had come.

Milton Humason in 1955. Humason's technical skill was key to Hubble's research.

The Hubbles had just returned to England from the Continent when they received word that Virginia James Hubble, Edwin's mother, had died of heart failure on July 26, 1934. Edwin had lost his father while he was still a student at Oxford. Jennie, a seventy-year-old widow, had been living in Louisiana with Edwin's younger brother Bill.

Edwin had almost completely cut himself off from his family since his days in the army. His infrequent letters home were not saved. Grace never did meet her in-laws. Whenever any of Edwin's brothers or sisters came west on vacation, he planned to meet them at his office or at a club or restaurant for dinner. None were invited to his home. It was as if Edwin were embarrassed by his family. Betsy, the youngest of the seven Hubble children, wondered if he might feel a little guilty that he had never contributed toward his mother's financial support. Yet to Grace's parents, he was a fine and caring husband to their daughter and one "who had made them all proud."

ANOTHER WAR

Hubble's frequent trips abroad were cut short by war in Europe in 1939. Again Hubble urged the United States to come to the aid of her allies. The issue was resolved soon enough when Japan attacked Pearl Harbor, and the United States was drawn into World War II.

Suddenly Caltech was under guard. Mount Wilson was turned into an observation post. Weather reports were confidential, and blackout regulations were strict. Grace enrolled in a first aid class, and Edwin applied for a job in the military.

He was asked to be head of the ballistics research program at the Aberdeen Proving Ground in Maryland. He later joked that he had had to go to the encyclopedia to look up the word *ballistic,* but he discovered it was an important job requiring far-reaching scientific research. All types of ammunition were tested. Accurate firing tables were calculated. The team studied the second-by-second behavior of a bomb released 3 miles (4.8 km) before its target from an overhead bomber. Tracing the speed of machine-gun bullets and designing shapes of new rockets were all part of the job. High-speed cameras were a necessity. The design of bombsights was a priority. It was not the theoretical analysis of figures Edwin had been used to, but practical, hands-on mathematics.

Hubble was offered the position as a civilian specialist. The problem here was that he was not eligible for military housing. Grace came with him on his first trip to Maryland to hunt for a place to live. None was found, and she was disconsolate when Edwin urged her to return to Pasadena until he could make some arrangements for them. Even hotel accommodations were unavailable, and Edwin had to share a room with another employee at the post.

MODEST ACCOMMODATIONS

Almost a year later, Hubble found a solution to their problem. Aberdeen is located on one of the islands off the shore of Maryland. Among the island's few structures was a small shack. It was empty, and for an obvious reason: it was in deplorable condition. There was one room and a bath downstairs and a tiny kitchen with a fireplace. The upstairs had been left abandoned because of a leaky roof and an assortment of

Hubble monitors a wind tunnel test at Aberdeen Proving Ground.

This shack near Aberdeen Proving Ground became the Hubble's home from 1942–1945. It was in such disrepair it was nicknamed the "haunted house."

strange creatures flying and crawling about. Edwin wrote to Grace urging her to come before someone else found this treasure.

Grace rushed to pack. She had been desperately lonely for her husband, and this was the answer to her prayers. When she saw what her prayers had brought about, however, she was truly shocked. She did not voice her disapproval but immediately set about trying to renovate the place. Edwin was so busy with his job that all was left up to her.

In later life, she wrote that it had always

amazed her that a man who spent hours checking the wires and mechanics of a telescope was unable to change a light bulb at home. With plenty of time on her hands, with nothing to do except read the bundle of books she had brought with her and scrub floors, she soon had the place in livable, definitely not luxurious, condition. Cooking was done on a two-burner hot plate. Heat was provided by a coal stove referred to as "Little Filthy." The problem of mice in the kitchen was solved by acquiring a cat, who proceeded to give birth to a litter of kittens. The problem that couldn't be taken care of was the sound of continuous explosions that rattled the windows and nerves, but to be together again was worth the many problems and inconveniences.

Toward the end of the war Grace and Edwin were able to spend a few days in Washington, D.C. When they returned, they were met by a captain with the disturbing news that their "Little Filthy" had caused a serious fire. Workmen had been rushed to the scene to make repairs, and within two weeks the appearance of the interior walls looked much better than they had even before the fire. Grace noted that they should have set the fire a bit earlier.

The outcome of the war now seemed obvious. The Allies were on the offensive on all fronts. Edwin was anxious to get back to his real work at the observatory and bemoaned the fact that so much time had been lost.

The news of Hiroshima and the atom bomb came as a deadly shock. Although Hubble's political views were very conservative, he was one of the few scientists who spoke out to urge that all atomic weapons be scrapped and that no more experimentation in this field be conducted. He felt the horror of what might yet come. He voiced his opinions whenever he had an audience and wrote to newspapers about what he called "The War That Must Not Happen." He implored, "It must now be world government or no world, one world or none." His views surprised some of his friends who felt that the discovery of nuclear energy was indeed a blessing.

When asked how he combined his religious beliefs with what he was seeing in the heavens, he answered, "The whole thing is so much bigger than I am, and I can't understand it, so I just trust myself to it, and forget about it."

"The whole thing is so much bigger than I am, and I can't understand it, so I just trust myself to it, and forget about it."

CHAPTER ELEVEN

THE GIANT TELESCOPE

During the war, construction of the Palomar Observatory had been put on hold. With the war's end, work on the giant 200-inch (508-cm) telescope resumed. Hubble returned to Mount Wilson and eagerly awaited the completion of the telescope.

Like everyone else, Hubble stopped almost every day at the Caltech optical laboratory to check on the polishing of the telescope's huge mirror. Finally, in November 1947, it was announced that the mirror was ready to be taken to the mountain. There was concern that someone would attempt to sabotage the event. Threatening letters had been received at the Caltech office. Every precaution to protect the valuable "giant eye" was being taken. A sixteen-wheel diesel truck accompanied by a police escort provided the transportation. It was a two-day, 33-mile (53-km) trip.

When combined with the 55-foot-long (17-

meter-long) barrel of the telescope, the entire instrument weighed in at 500 tons. The task of mounting such a gigantic piece of machinery so that it could be easily moved within the observatory dome and aimed with absolute precision created a monumental problem. The solution turned out to be quite simple. The entire mechanism was mounted on a horseshoe-shaped base. A well-

Palomar Observatory

advertised brand of lanolin-rich hair oil was forced through five bearing pads so that the instrument was actually floating on a thin film of liquid. So little friction was produced that the entire telescope could be moved with a small motor about the size used for an ordinary sewing machine. The dome itself was made in sections like the petals of a flower and could be closed and opened at the touch of a button.

Astronomers no longer had to climb ladders to reach the eyepiece. Instead, they could don electrically heated coveralls and step into an elevator that would take them to the observation level. An intercom kept them in contact with the night attendant who set the controls in motion according to the directions he received from above. The telescope was synchronized with the movement of the earth, so once the target was locked in view, the search through outer space could begin.

The final dedication took place on June 3, 1948. The giant instrument was named the Hale Telescope after George Ellery Hale, the great astronomer who had been a mentor to Hubble and given so much to the field of astronomy. But the initial use of the great telescope was delayed another six months for further adjustments. Hubble was given the honor of processing the first plates. They bear his initials and the numbers one

This image of a variable nebula, processed by Hubble, was the first plate taken with the great Hale Telescope at Palomar.

through eight. Through the Hale Telescope, the Andromeda galaxy appeared three times as large and nine times as bright as what he had seen through the 100-inch (254-cm) telescope at Mount Wilson. There were complaints, however, that images were not as clear as they should be. Some further refinements had to be made. In May, the huge mirror was removed and lowered into a vacuum chamber on the lower level of the observatory for more polishing.

Palomar was closed for a few more months, an exasperating time. Hubble returned to Mount Wilson for more sightings, but then he and Grace headed across the Atlantic again for lectures and social events. Hubble was elected Honorary Fellow of Oxford University's Queen's College, the first Rhodes scholar to receive the honor. He was surrounded by reporters who asked him whether being able to see so much farther with the new telescope might not change his theory of an expanding universe. He replied, "I am not worried about theory." Then, when asked how he felt when he first looked through the giant eye, he admitted, "I thought I was blasé, but I got all excited about it."

"I am not worried about theory."

Some astronomers had come up with the theory that the red shift of stars' light coming from such great distances might be explained by the fact that the stars' energy had been depleted, "tired light" they called it. Hubble said that he did not expect to find such evidence, but if he did, the discovery would be quite as sensational as his first hypothesis. Meanwhile, Hubble's assistant Milton Humason was busy collecting data that continued to substantiate Hubble's original claims.

When not on speaking engagements, Edwin and Grace often vacationed at a lodge in Colorado. In July 1949, about a week into their stay, Hubble awoke in the middle of the night with severe chest pain, but did not disturb his wife until dawn. After sunrise, an alarmed Grace gave him a pain killer and summoned the ranch manager. Within hours, they started down the mountain to the nearest hospital in the town of Grand Junction, Colorado. It was late afternoon before they arrived, but Grace had phoned ahead before they left, and an emergency medical team was waiting for him.

FAILING HEALTH

An electrocardiogram showed that Hubble had indeed had a heart attack, but he seemed alert and certainly looked healthy with a tan he had acquired the month before, hiking on a mountain trail. On the fourth day, however, an even stronger attack occurred. Hubble was in extreme pain but never lost consciousness. Grace rarely left his side. He was kept in intensive care and monitored around the clock. Yet he was anxious to get back to Pasadena. Within a month, arrangements were made to take him by ambulance to the train station. It was near midnight when he was met by his personal physician, who, with the help of two orderlies, transferred him to his second-floor bedroom at home.

His recovery was slow, but he was anxious to get back to work. The doctors had warned that it would be dangerous for him to work at the high altitude of Mount Palomar, at least for the time being, and he was to give up pipe smoking. Grace tried to keep his condition a secret from the public. Even the staff at the observatory did not know how close to death he had come. When reporters called to find out about his health, they were told that reports of the seriousness of his condition had been much exaggerated.

By mid-October, when he finally did get to his office, his tan had faded and his coworkers were shocked at how he had aged. Grace continued to try to keep his spirits up and helped by answering all the correspondence addressed both to their home address and his office. Two years before, Hubble had been appointed to a seat on the board of trustees of the Huntington Library and Art Gallery. It was a job that carried little responsibility but much prestige. Edwin enjoyed walking through the gardens and spending afternoons picking out choice volumes to study. He had often been criticized for having exaggerated his literary knowledge and tastes, but there would have been no need at this time in his life to impress others. He enjoyed a wide range of subjects.

He asked to have reports sent to him on what was being done on the mountain. It was at this time that a young astronomer, Allan Sandage, was appointed to act as his observing assistant. Sandage proved he was up to the job, but as he said in later life, he couldn't recall which was the most frightening to him—Hubble or the universe.

BACK ON THE MOUNTAIN

When medical approval was finally made for Edwin's first run on the mountain, Grace went with him. She occupied one of the guest cottages while Edwin took a room in the all-male "Monastery," as it was called. She constantly worried about his health, but she knew she couldn't keep him away from his beloved telescope. Hubble himself must have known that his time was growing short. He remarked to one of his friends. "You know, if I can have two more years, I feel I can accomplish as much as I can expect to during my lifetime."

With the help of the ever faithful Humason and the enthusiastic Sandage, Hubble still managed to keep an eye on the work of probing deep

Hubble in England in 1950

space. Humason had measured the velocity of one galaxy that was receding at the velocity of about one-fifth the speed of light, an amazing figure. It would take other, more sophisticated technology in the future to pry farther into space.

"You know, if I can have two more years, I feel I can accomplish as much as I can expect to during my lifetime."

CHAPTER TWELVE

THE LAST HORIZON

Hubble had recovered sufficiently to enjoy his sport of fishing in solitude. Grace enjoyed horseback riding, so it was only in the evenings at the dinner hour that they joined other guests at their favorite lodge.

They took one more trip to Europe, aboard the *Mauritania,* in April 1953. Edwin was scheduled to give a special lecture before the Royal Astronomical Society. Grace had asked that there be no questions following the talk for fear it would tire her husband too much. She was very careful to see that Edwin followed all doctor's rules, with a few of her own thrown in for good measure.

They were also invited to attend a formal event hosted by Queen Elizabeth II, who at the time was only twenty-six years old. Grace was very impressed with how the queen handled her crowd of admirers. There was a certain warmth to her greeting, even though she could not have known half the people present. The Duke of Edinburgh, the queen's husband, arranged a reception in the old observatory, which had since been turned into a museum. Again, Hubble was asked to present a lecture, which he did with the aid of slides taken with the new 200-inch (508-cm) telescope. He remarked quietly, "This is the last horizon." The audience burst into applause.

"This is the last horizon."

He then returned to Scotland, where he again put aside time for fishing. It was a standing joke that he was always able to schedule his important meetings in areas featuring good fishing during the season when the trout were biting best.

A FINAL TRIP TO PALOMAR

When they returned home, Hubble prepared his notes and his equipment for a trip to Palomar on September 1. It was his first run in eleven months. He was excited about the prospect of three whole nights in his favorite chair high up in the dome. He was not able to dominate the hours of viewing as he had done in the past. There were now more astronomers listed on the faculty. Time had to be shared. It aggravated him at times, but much of his definitive work was done in his office sorting through plates that had been taken previously, mathematically testing some of his more imaginative theories. He also spent a great deal of time answering mail that came to him from around the world. He found it stimulating to

*Hubble in the observing cage of the
Hale Telescope at Palomar*

share ideas and debate puzzling topics with fellow astronomers, many of whom he had never met.

On September 28, 1953, his wife picked him up at his office so that they could have lunch together at their home. As the car was pulling into their driveway he suddenly lost consciousness. Grace called out to Berta, their housekeeper, who immediately summoned help on the phone. By the time the doctor arrived, it was evident that Hubble's heart had stopped beating. He had suffered a fatal stroke.

Grace was devastated by his death. He had seemed so healthy and full of enthusiasm on their last trip. She had come to hope that all danger was past. She refused to give interviews and kept her grief a private affair. There was no memorial service, no formal funeral. It is said that his ashes were scattered near the observatory. No one seems to be able to substantiate this claim. It is only known that there is no gravestone to mark the name of Edwin Hubble.

Instead a mightier memorial, one that would have pleased him more than any other, was dedicated on the day the Hubble Space Telescope blasted into orbit.

1889	Edwin Powell Hubble is born on November 20 to John Powell Hubble and Virginia Lee James Hubble in Marshfield, Missouri.
1896	Hubble is devastated by death of sister Virginia on January 14.
1906	At age 16, Hubble enters the University of Chicago.
1910	In September, Hubble is awarded a Rhodes scholarship to study in England, and he decides to study law.
1914	During the summer, Hubble is accepted as a graduate student of astronomy at the University of Chicago.
1914	In August, Hubble is elected a member of the American Astronomical Society.
1917	Hubble receives his doctoral degree in the spring and immediately joins the United States Army.
1917	On August 5, Hubble is made Commander of the 2nd Battalion of the 343rd Infantry.

1919	Hubble returns to the United States in August and accepts a position at the Mount Wilson Observatory.
1924	Hubble marries Grace Burke Leib on February 26.
1924	An article is appears in the November 25 issue of the *New York Times* publicizing Hubble's findings on "Island Universes."
1926	The Hubbles move into their home in Pasadena. It is a gift from Grace's parents.
1931	In January, the Hubbles entertain Albert Einstein and his wife in their home. They become friends.
1942	Hubble is asked to head the ballistics research program at the Aberdeen Proving Ground in Maryland.
1948	The great Hale Telescope is dedicated in Palomar on June 3. Months later, Hubble is given the honor of exposing the first plates.
1949	Hubble has a heart attack in July.
1953	In April, Hubble presents lectures during his last trip to Europe.
1953	Edwin Hubble suffers a fatal stroke on September 28.
1990	The Hubble Space Telescope is launched aboard the space shuttle *Discovery* on April 14.
1993	The Hubble Space Telescope is repaired by a crew aboard the space shuttle *Endeavor* in December.
1997	Insulation on the exterior of the Hubble Space Telescope is repaired by a crew aboard the space shuttle *Discovery* in February.

NOTE ON SOURCES

During his lifetime, Edwin Hubble was known to many people in different walks of life, and rarely did they agree on their description of his character and personality. Rather than trying to find a general consensus, I have presented different points of view at different stages of his life and career.

Hubble's family has left proud accounts of him that are surely prejudiced to some degree, but no one could have achieved such tremendous accomplishments without the single-minded persistence Hubble showed all through his life.

The most personal assessment of Hubble was made by his wife Grace Burke Hubble in journals and notes that are now part of the Henry E. Huntington Library in San Marino, California.

Some accounts by Hubble's coworkers describe him as aloof and inclined to brag about his accomplishments. Yet he rarely bragged about his academic career. His boasting usually involved his alleged heroism during war years and, for example, a rather elaborate (and perhaps dubious) description of his having fought off bandits in the north woods of Wisconsin in his youth.

Hubble was much impressed by his stay in England, and his detractors made fun of his speedily acquired British accent.

Edwin Hubble was never one to isolate himself within the confines of his academic role. He enjoyed being the center of attention and liked to surround himself with those who had achieved attention in other fields. Charlie Chaplin, a youthful Walt Disney, Clark Gable, and author Aldous Huxley were as likely to be dinner guests as Albert Einstein, who came to discuss the composition of the universe.

There is no doubt that Hubble was a dedicated scientist who could put in long hours of cold, lonely observation. His skill lay in being able to interpret the statistical information that resulted from those hours. With the exception of his trusted technician Milton Humason, Hubble rarely worked closely with other sceintists. He was not considered a team player.

Many reference books give the bare facts of Hubble's life and studies. A much more detailed account is found in the biography written by Dale E. Christianson titled *Edwin Hubble: Mariner of the Nebulae*. Another fine source is the chapter on Hubble included in *The Astronomers* by Donald Goldsmith.

Perhaps the most exciting reference materials are the newspaper and magazine articles written at the time Hubble first published his "island universes" theory. These articles summarize Hubble's findings, presenting the the general public with a universe in which our Milky Way is but one of a thousand (now revised to several billion) other galaxies. This changed forever how we would look at our own small world.

Books for Young Readers

Camp, Carole Ann. *American Astronomers: Searchers and Wonderers*. Springfield, NJ: Enslow Publishers,1995.

Matloff, Gregory L. *Telescope Power: Fantastic Activities and Easy Projects for Young Astronomers*. New York: J. Wiley, 1993.

Moeschl, Richard. *Exploring the Sky: Projects for Beginning Astronomers*. Chicago: Chicago Review Press, 1993.

Porcellino, Michael R. *A Young Astronomer's Guide to the Night Sky*. Blue Ridge Summit, PA: TAB Books, 1991.

Ridpath, Ian. *The Young Astronomer's Handbook*. New York: Arco Publishing, 1984.

Vogt, Gregory. *The Hubble Space Telescope*. Brookfield, CT.: Millbrook Press, 1992.

Books for Older Readers

Barbree, Jay, and Martin Caidin. *A Journey Through Time: Exploring the Universe with the Hubble*

Space Telescope. New York: Penguin Studio Books, 1995.

Christianson, Gale E. *Edwin Hubble: Mariner of the Nebulae.* New York: Farrar, Straus, Giroux, 1995.

Goodwin, Simon. *Hubble's Universe: A Portrait of Our Cosmos.* New York: Viking Penguin, 1997.

Hubble, Edwin Powell. *The Realm of the Nebulae.* New York: Dover Publications, 1991.

Petersen, Carolyn Collins, and John C. Brandt. *Hubble Vision: Astronomy with the Hubble Space Telescope.* Cambridge: Cambridge University Press, 1995.

INTERNET RESOURCES

Due to the changeable nature of the Internet, sites appear and disappear very quickly. These resources offered useful information on Edwin Hubble and astronomy at the time of publication.

Mount Wilson Observatory
http://www.mtwilson.edu/
Visit the home of the 100-inch (245-cm) telescope that allowed Hubble to pry into the depths of outer space. This site includes articles, biographies of key people associated with the observatory, and a timeline marking important events. The site also includes an archive of historical images, including one of Hubble looking through the large telescope. The site provides information about requesting time on the large telescope— for the price of $1,300 per night.

Palomar Observatory
http://astro.caltech.edu/observatories/palomar/
This observatory houses the huge Hale Telescope,

which is still an important research tool. The site, maintained by the Caltech Astronomy Department, includes instrumentation data, a section on visitor information, an informative tourist brochure, an archive of historical images, and a gallery of images from around the site and in the sky.

Space Shuttle Site
http://shuttle.nasa.gov
This site includes information about past and present space shuttle missions including those involving the Hubble Space Telescope. Check out the archive of images from space shuttle missions.

Space Telescope Science Institute
http://www.stsci.edu/
The Space Telescope Science Institute is the astronomical research center responsible for operating the Hubble Space Telescope. Many of Hubble's theories are being substantiated and revised based on the data gathered by the Hubble Space Telescope. This Web site includes information about the telescope, including the latest news, technical information, and a detailed history. This site also includes an up-to-date archive of space images taken by the telescope.

Yerkes Observatory
http://astro.uchicago.edu/Yerkes.html
The Yerkes observatory, affiliated with the University of Chicago, is the home of the largest refractor telescope in the world. It was here that Hubble received his undergraduate education. The site includes information about visiting Yerkes, a virtual tour of the observatory, and descriptions of past and current projects.

INDEX

ABOUT THE AUTHOR

Mary Virginia Fox graduated from Northwestern University and now lives near Madison, Wisconsin, conveniently located across the lake from the state capital and the University of Wisconsin. She is the author of forty-one books for young people and a score of feature articles for adult publications.